Sorrows of the Sun

Sogol Sur

SKYSCRAPER PUBLICATIONS

Published by Skyscraper Publications Limited
20 Crab Tree Close, Bloxham, OX15 4SE
www.skyscraperpublications.com

First published 2017

A CIP catalogue record for this book is available
from the British Library.

ISBN-13: 978-1-911072-23-2

Cover concept and design by Sin,
additional design by Rebecca Lynch.

Designed and typeset
by Chandler Book Design

Printed in the United Kingdom
by CPI

DEDICATION

To my mother

who died too soon, too quickly

Yet will never leave me

A glorious commander, an ecstatic mentor,

and a tearful lover

A caring and beautiful thinker

who taught me Nietzsche and

threw me in the arms of philosophy

when I was a clueless teenager

CONTENTS

Foreword
Julia Bell

Pouran Farrokhzad, sister of the iconoclastic feminist poet Forugh Farrokhzad, said playfully in a 2009 interview:

'In general all Iranians are in love, in other words, hot blooded, the reason is the sun that shines directly over Iran. When the sun shines so strongly ... love is more passionate and when love is more passionate it gives rise to poetry.'

In this new collection the sun illuminates the passionate young poet – Sogol Sur - who lives between London and Tehran. The sun is almost a metaphor for the poet who is also very aware of the sorrows to which she is witness. Across every line of this accomplished and surprising first collection the pains of love and grief and nationality are analysed from a new point of view. Making reference to classical Persian poetry but humming with the rhythms of the London streets, this poetry speaks with a luminous and affecting honesty. In one long poem – *On the Phone* – the narrator interrogates her mother, a rousing confession not just of hot-blooded fierceness, but also of inquisition and melancholy.

In another, *Infected Parrot*, the poetry chafes against cultural expectations, against the way in which in London the poet is expected to be a bird with different, more exotic, kinds of feathers.

Love or its absence also features heavily as a subject – in *The Leather Sun* or *Game* – where the problems of the romantics are addressed. Matters of gender identity and sexuality are fluid and fluent, sex is decadent, love disappointing. Life is equivocal, urban, inbetween. And threaded throughout is the figure of the poet's mother and the grief of her loss. *Black Lace* for example with its stark and moving simplicity.

In each piece is an articulation of a problem, or a mood, or a question – being in cool, rainy England, compared to hot, noisy Teheran – and in between is the poet, admiring of beautiful boys and girls, decadent, sometimes solipsistic, always surprising, new.

Infected Parrot

I have no place to stay.
My bed is overflowing with boys,
my mind with girls.
'Gender is a performance'
I repeat, like an infected parrot.

I am an eternally inebriated animal,
hence my bed is hollow, my mind an asylum
filled with refugees who will be deported
back, back, back.
To war.

But we have no place to go.
My bed is broken and
even though my mind is blooming
like a European Museum of Contemporary Art
I know I cannot stay.

I do not know about the refugees,
I am an international student,
paying, not to be a threat
to national security.
Look at my exotic feathers.

I am an international parrot
my bed is filled with dysfunctional languages
with German philosophy, British fiction, and
    Persian poetry
with murderous grammar rules
with alcoholic European dreams.

I learn things, and repeat them until
my beak bleeds,
And I write with my blood
poems about painless pleasure.
And I shall always lie and repeat:

I am not political. I am a woman of pleasure,
a cold lake full of colourful shells.
I'm not wounded I'm not bothered by the bloodshed

by the crushing cages of the mad Middle East
and the ruthless borders of enlightened Europe.
All I care about is who to slaughter
in my solipsistic bed tonight.

On the Phone

Mother, today your strong hands look
    wrinkled
and you don't remember my name.
How can you tell me
where you hid the weapons?

Mother, I'm afraid I have some bad news
    for you
— as always:
I killed someone today.
Out of pure pleasure.

Mother, tell me, where are we going now?
Take me somewhere else and tell me if
we lost our Syrian friends to chemical weapons
or bad luck?

Or are we fortunate?
After all, we weren't bombed
and sometimes we drink Christ's blood
in our sunny basements.

Mother, where are we now?
Where are you? And where am I?
Do you still cover your hair with a floral scarf?
Do you still pray to God?

Mother, what are we doing? Are we making
    stew and rice
for the poor so we won't feel guilty afterwards?
Or have we become poor ourselves? Stoned
    and sanctioned
and isolated like guinea pigs?

Mother, should I stop whining? And consider
    us lucky
that we don't have as many honour killings
as Arabs and Pakis? But I can't feel fortunate
I feel bad for them, for every one of us.

Mother, tell me why we should abhor Arabs?
Are we really better than they are? Please,
tell me we are. We have Persian poetry, Persian
    carpets, and Persian cats.
All they have is oil, Islam, and America.

And yet I confess sometimes, surreptitiously,
I read Mahmoud Darwish and cry.
Mother, let's face it I am one of those
    weak fighters,
destined to fail.

A country could never be proud of me, I could
    only be a spy
Nobody needs me and I don't need anybody
I don't need any country
I am free and strong. I don't belong

Mother, I fancy suicide too often, too much
It makes me calm.
Mother, I cannot care that suicide is a sin
I want to go to hell and violate all my friends.

Mother, please, don't be ashamed that
    our government
is supporting Assad. My therapist convinced
    me I
should not be ashamed of the things that
    aren't my fault,
and according to him nothing has ever been
    my fault.

Mother, tell me the truth for once. Have
    you sold
our weapons to feed the poor and buy
    black scarves?

Mother, why do you act like a prophet?
Like a victorious warrior?
Why don't you accept we have lost the war?
'Which war?' You ask, as if you had no idea

Mother, don't act. Not for me.
'Iraq?' You ask as if you were ignorant,
    innocent, and young.

'No, not that one, they were as weak as us.'
The Other war.

'Elaborate.' You say like a sadistic teacher.
'The war against everything and everyone.'
Yes, mother, there was a war.
And we lost because we were right.

Mother, I confess I'm not impressed with
    your strength.
My therapist implied I should not be so
    power-obsessed
And I'm trying to be cured by his false
    interpretations because
I like his neck. I meant to only tell you about
    his neck, but–

Mother, is America going to attack us?
Did you hear their new speech?
But maybe they have a right to loathe us
Our government threatened them first.

Do you think I'm crazy?

When I asked this question of my therapist
whilst staring into his sorry eyes, he took
    my hands
and squeezed them with an ideal pressure,
a white slave with a fetish for dark hair.

Then I informed him I did not need therapy
and I never did. 'I need your neck.'
I finally showered him with the truth he was after
'I need power.' I guided him to my broken bed.

Mother, I know it does not make you proud
    of me
but I swear to you, my only prophet, it was okay
he was sweet in bed and out of bed
until I opened my closet and showed him
    our weapons.

I need to protect our weapons. Mother, I want
    to protect your sacred wrinkles.

And like Antigone, I want to bury the corpses
    of our Syrian friends.
Mother, living people bore me. Shaky like a
    pot of jelly
afraid to say if they prefer tea or coffee.

Do they fight like us? Do they care about Syria?
Mother, I have news for you: I have stopped
    caring about Syria, too.

Mother, these days, I don't talk. Nobody
    really talks. Except about the weather
and the importance of milk in their tea,
grilled sausages and cheese and how well
    singers can sing.
But mother, let me tell you a secret: singers
    are the only people who can't sing.

Mother, yesterday I drew a mosque. Then I
    threw it away as I got scared.
I will not say what I thought. This morning,
    I drew my therapist and

masturbated on his picture; it was nice.
    My drawing was nice.
My masturbation was nice. Everything was nice.

I recalled the way I shot him with one of
    our guns
his blood – the colour of my nail varnish:
    blue and calm
on my pink, floral sheets. I licked it - it
    tasted raw.
It tasted like Syria.

Mother, do you think the police will find me?
Do we have enough weapons? And enough
    time to die?
Mother, I feel safe. His corpse is safe. The
    world is a safe place.
I'm a good person, like you always asked me
    to be.

Mother, I don't murder for pleasure, I have
    morals.

I use clean guns and I sympathise with the
poor.
Mother, I'm a pacifist, can't you see? Coming
from the Middle East,
I'm advocating peace; aren't you proud of me?

Family Resemblance

Was it you or your sister
who caressed my neck
on that sunny day.
I don't remember
- you two look the same -
except that your eyes are brighter
and your sister is dead.

Black Lace

I was riding my scarlet horse towards the skies
    of glory
when an arrow was shot from nowhere,
nowhere that has colour.
My horse died. And the golden skies turned
    into the colour of my blood.

The black lace kimono I used to wear to haunt
    my lovers,
now I wear to mourn my mother
whose tempest of death drowned the racing
    yacht of my life and
withered the flower of my youth.

Finally, I fathomed
why Jacob lost his eyesight.

Game

Level One: Beauty
I have fucked them all,
Them,
Them, the pretty men who walk in beauty
who walk in my head, who stroll the restless
    streets of my intoxicated psyche
waving their tight bums from left to right
like a bunch of royal cats.

Their cheekbones are my mountains of
    pleasure which I ascend until
I reach the peak
the peak of their beauty
and my game until
I'm bored, bored
bored.

As soon as the sun starts melting in
    their eyes
I leave
I leave them
howling
falling
begging by my bed.

You have to vanish, like all surreptitious lovers
My beautiful boys
I have to go although the sun is melting in
    your eyes
و خروشید در چشمان شما ذوب میشود
and your necks are saplings in the dark.
و گردن شما نهالیست درخشان در باغی
تاریک

Level Two: Persian
I am dark
and my mind is black
but my privilege isn't white
it is mad. My madness is my privilege

This is how I shall mistreat you behind my mask
     of lunacy
made of logic and repression.
This is what happens:
At the end of the day, you sell your intelligence
     to the system and
purchase some madness to put on your face
like expensive make-up, it justifies all your wrongs
and in the morning, you spread my madness on
     your toast and bread
and digest it with tea.
(Interesting fact: we, Iranians, don't pour milk
     in our tea
this is our privilege.
Milkless tea
Dark tea
Black tea)

Level Three: Stage Four
Oh, my shiny darlings,
Once you drink my frenzy, and my cloudy tea
     in my sunny country

Once you worship my shark teeth, you become
just like me:
invincible and incurable
like stage 4 cancer

A Fairy Took Me Hunting in Sexpring

Tell my Asian angel to take off her black dress
and wear her coral kimono: I'm taking her
   hunting.
Tell her to wipe off her gothic make up, wear
   her golden
eyeshadow, cherry lipstick. I'm taking her to
   the forest.

Winter has wept enough, he should stay away -
   like all expired lovers
there was a time when he could excite me.
Legs long and slender, cheekbones, the finest
   knives
tears sweet ice in my mouth, kisses freezing
   my skin.

My angel is seducing me, singing in my ears
eyes greener than the sea, sun-lit nights and
    lustful mornings.
Winter smelled like lengthy essays about politics,
but then I was a strayed cat myself content
    inside my burning car

Asian angel, choke me in your arms and tell
    me why
I was once in love with winter and stray cats
    under sweaty cars.
Caress my cheeks some more and let me shoot
    those birds
who admire you with their screams. They're
    disturbing our peace.

My Favourite Painting

My face is crimson and my favourite object
is vibrating,
Neon red, reminding me of your head
between my waiting thighs like the promise of
    rain in
the amber sky of Tehran.

The Leather Sun

It is five a.m. and there is a woman growing
inside my head. Not like a tumor –
but a flower that feeds on power
she makes me tremble

Words devour me. I open my mouth,
thirsty for more, this is a sweet-tasting storm
I know someday this bed of hers
will be my comfortable tomb

For now, this monstrous bed is a gilded ship,
a surreptitious ship, my shelter,
I stare into her eyes until they are the sun and
I melt, melt, melt. It is true:

I am like Icarus in my ridiculous ambition and
    lack of abstinence

in my love of flight, height, and light.
But she calls me Napoleon, and laughs
in my ears with a choking sound

her leather scent fills my throbbing nostrils
    like cocaine,
she kisses my neck and worships my
    shamelessness, she says
I am arrogant and licks my lips. Outside,
    the sun,
a blood red orange, waiting to be peeled by us.

Understanding Anna

The day I moved into this room, I
shouted, 'Anna Karenina!'
The window opened to the senile rail,
a train screaming under.

Little did I know that soon I would
encounter Vronsky too
that soon
I would be ruined.

My Vronsky is seven years younger
than me. Pale as the autumn wind, hissing
in my ears, his delicate bones beckoning me
    to treachery,
I cannot want him. Alas! I desire him

At night, alone, listening to my dark window

shattered by the roar of train, my bed is
made of shards of glass, I am
torturously cognizant that he is not an error —
    but a disaster.

Alas! I cannot stop,
his eternally moist lips a heart-shaped lake
in which my anxious skin sinks. My guilt
    subsides in
the sea of his navy blue eyes, half-open, as
    though I am a half-serious desire.

After saying 'good night, my love.' to my
    partner on the phone, I
invite Vronsky to my room,
it is midnight again. His steps hasty, yet cold
the train howls, wading through my Russian
    window.

The Believers

I was striving to be a god when I was a child
not the kind of god my mother worshipped and
my father despised; a kinder and stronger god,
the sort of god my father wouldn't question.
The man of science believed in Darwin and I
    confess
I understood neither science nor God;
but I wanted to become Darwin just to please
    my father.
'How sad! How Freudian!
What a tedious cliché for a useless, little girl
to be in love with her father.'
I can still hear my mother thunder
after praying in her chador wrapped around
her bending body like a grey garden
kneeling before her unforgiving God.

Sometimes Our Persona Melts in the Sun

You and I talk about how your wife tortures
    your son,
then you cry, dropping your head on my
    shoulder, and mumble, 'I'm tired.'
I try my best to sip my ice tea, bewildered
    and paralyzed.

You and I talk about how we should seduce
    younger guys,
endorphin wraps around our necks - choking us,
my hands are sweaty, hence I'm ashamed.

You say you would lick my sweat if it weren't
    for the eyes
around us in the café, on the streets, in our
    rooms, on our walls,
the petty gods, eternally bored, praying

we would cross the line, so they could punish
    us some more.
You and I always in the garden of our far
    away café
We have no house we are not homeless, just
    unhomed,

sharing houses with people we don't know:
our parents, our teachers, our partners,
    our prophets,
our boundaries, our Imams, our bad luck.

You and I have always talked about
Oscar Wilde, and Ahmad Shamloo, about
    Brecht, and Annie Baker
We have always lost.

You crave to be the devil, but I know you are
    just a weeping saint.
I want to look at you when you talk. And
    when you don't talk
when you play with your summery, little son

even when you argue with your falling wife
who knows your so-called secret. Why shouldn't
    she argue?
Why shouldn't she threaten you?

Why shouldn't she abuse your son to make up
for all the times you kissed men behind her back?
For every time you told me I am your love, your
    only friend, your confidant.

Do you think she's wary of my strange
    existence?
'That annoying little girl, so full of herself.
Why are you friends anyway?'

Our little gods judge us and we fail and we
    break and we fall,
but you lift me up, and I pick you up among
    negative HIV tests,
and hedonistic jokes,

we are always scared of our final punishment:

STDs, execution, shame, exile, forced suicide,
    what is it?
Give it to us already.

You and I, the dark lesson for the future nation
so they will always obey, they will always buy lies.
We are also frightened of being found out that
    we are not evil

that we cry in the dark, and laugh in the light
that your fast car is just a façade of your suicide
we get drunk on Arak and we look as though
    we want to fuck all the pretty boys.

We are here for the sake of fuck that is the
    plan, the plot, our persona
whereas we only want to bang our heads against
the sharp edges of the festive table and die

or not die, maybe survive, perhaps spend some
    time in a silver hospital
where nurses are nonjudgmental —

they'll even sleep with us if we ask them with
   some charm

where you're not married, and I'm not stuck
where it is raining, and this aggressive sun is gone.
Now, I am standing in the dark.

I lost my sight in the constant presence of the
   sun which
has always been too bright for my eyes.
My weak eyes. My wicked eyes.

I know you are standing somewhere near me,
as blind and as lost as me, hoping you will
   drown, soon,
in a rainy sea where there is no sun, but your son,

no god, apart from our love.
I can feel you're breathing near me, you are
   almost living
Tell me where you are.

V

Neon blue toe nails on pale feet
dead fish in a dried lake
pants pulled down, top pulled up
V is on.

Push your lovers under the carpet, instead of drugs,
sniff their scented ashes to stay healthy and ecstatic.
Dig a grave for your willing prey, for expired
    blunders
Victory is on its way

Inhale it like you inhaled boys' necks in the rain
V is calling you like gold tigers in rainy
    forests and
withered flowers on your virginal windowpanes
when you were sixteen.

Real Boys Are Made of Dreams

You are a real boy, made of dreams
you smell like English rain and melting
    chocolate, and
your skin is so soft that when I touch it
a thousand innocent seas open their mouths
and drown me

Your name starts with C,
and I call you sea to your dismay,
but I don't say the reasons, you think I do
    not care
you gorgeously suffer, your cheeks blood red,
    you moan, you roar, you beg
calling me your torturer, opening your heart-
    shaped mouth for more torment.

Boy, you are a fresh flower
I count your petals every night to make sure
    they're all mine.
Last week when the sun was the only sadist in
    the sky
you turned twenty, and I recall with a nonstop
    smile that I took your virginity
I reek of victory.

The most hedonistic win that will eventually
    ruin me.
Your friends despise me
so does your repressed society
but you say I am your dream.
Boy, you are a gift, my reward for being deeply
    obedient to the gods of pleasure.

You want me to spit on you
I do not dare to stain such beauty, I do not
    wish to make the gods angry.
I ask you to read me your juvenile poems,
you read three lines, and then you pull down
    your dark hoodie on your light face,
declaring you can't.

We are in a shed, deep in the dark,
you high on drugs, I high on you, the knife
    of life
you tell me your dad is a true poet, your hero,
more important to you than Wallace Stevens
I sniff your neck, letting my hands rummage
    through your dark trousers

your breaths as loud as the whistle of the train
    that will one day run over this shed.
I close my eyes,
thinking my dad is my hero too, not only more
    important than
Wallace Stevens,
but more so than everyone else.

I am a dragon daughter.
I was born in the year of the dragon.
and dragons only relish flames. Boy, I have so
    much nonsense in my head to share
but I don't want to say anything to you apart
    from the tragic fact that
you are beautiful.

Winter Woman

You were born in winter and every other day,
    you behave like winter;
but when I get cold to the point that I almost
    escape you stop me,
staring into my eyes, and call me your
    Asian spring.
Yet when I take your hands and confess you're
    a warm castle of roses
in which I am lost, you snow, mentioning your
    ancient boyfriend.

Do I look like I care about irrelevant matters?
    I am my daddy's girl,
always getting what I want, never sick of war
    and love
and after all, you are right, I am an
    Asian spring

but do you know nothing about Asia or spring?
You European winter: arctic, glorious, shameless.

Do you not know that when we plan to conquer
    a castle
we don't care whether it snows or rains or even
    if there's thunder?
Have you not noticed when your thorny roses
    cut my fingers,
you end up drinking my tears? You, with
    your eighteenth century morality complex
    wrapped around your neck like a serpent.

Gold Rope

The gold rope they wrap around my neck has a
    name: 'commitment'.
Lovers are executors, murderers who hang you
    from the sky-blue ceiling
who let you writhe in pleasure first - an ecstatic
    pig unaware of its upcoming slaughter —
before offering you the black news buried in a
    gilded box called 'love'

Shame! They don't know me, will never know me.
My neck is thinner than my fingers
my neck welcomes, like-bites and wistful
    kisses, but
when they bring out their golden rope, calling
    it a gold chain,
my neck gets cold.

As I age, the snake of marriage slips away from
  my reach, like my mother
I am neither sad nor happy at hearing all my
  lovers chanting
calling my name, accusing my neck of being a
  'slut'
as their golden ropes weave through my past
  and future
I keep running, panting, falling in the gold
  corridors
of lust where my restless neck can finally rest,
  oblivious of the dresscode.

Sunlit Suicide in the Bathtub

I am sick. Mother murdered me
Can you make tea and make love to me?
There are thoughts stuck in my throat that won't
    let me breathe
and my hands are weeping
and my mother insists I'm obsessed with politics
did you make tea?

do you still fancy me: nude, on a rainy beach?
will you tell my mother that politics is nothing
    to me?
That to me, politics is as expired as that rancid
    meat in her fridge?
ask her to stop discussing politics with me
inform her that I'm more interested in counting
    numbers that don't exist.
Don't make tea, just leave me

Why are you stuck on me?
like chewed gum on a dry rock
like politics on my mother
like my thoughts on my throat
like your hands on my mind
But it was your words that made me blind.

Your eyes made me bleed but my blood is
    not horrific.
My blood is white like cum as innocent as
    your neck
Would you like some?
Where is my tea? In your dirty mug?
I have been stuck in this bath tub for years
    now, but I still feel unclean
I think I might be sick.

It could be the tea, the weak English tea that's
    made me sick.
But I admit I've always been sick.
I've always tormented my mother with
    my illness

I've always liked to listen to insects have sex
I want to plunge my nails in the garden of
    your neck
I want you to embrace me like a bathtub in spring.

I am sick.

I like to repeat something until my teeth break,
the paler your neck, the darker my lips
the water in this tub is either too hot or too
    cold which
makes me want to drown something - or
    someone.
I am sick; I relish the sight of your skin
but turn off the sun please, life under water is
    so serene.

This Time of the Year

The clouds are singing thunder again
the sky is drowning in the rain and the rain is
abusing my hair even though I promised the rain I
would love it to death.

This time of the year I wish I
had betrayed you again and again
with the rain caressing my skin, injecting life
    in me
making me dizzy with pictures of pleasure.

I know I should have betrayed you,
under the sun, under the rain, in my lazy flat,
    on my waiting bed;
It's written in the holy books, and scientific
    essays that I should've betrayed you.
It would've been the only way to commit.

Betrayal, the only way to admit you're right
to claim you're not insane and not to condemn
  your hallucinations.

Oh, how I wish your accusations were right,
  indeed, they are lovely
and bright, I should've made love to
  numerous people,
all glistening, non-accusing, waiting for me,
the promise of spring carved on their
  crystal necks.

I should've sacrificed you in the temple of
  pleasure,
Should've buried you alive in the beauty of
  others.

Alas! I was too late. I am always late as I am
    busy thinking who
to betray and regretting when I murder my
    opportunities

Perhaps, your accusations are right, perhaps,
    I am a traitor by nature.
Treachery excites me and you sticking to me,
    and stalking me bores me,
in fact it terrifies me. Oh, my beautiful darling
    you repel me
like rancid milk force-fed to me in my
    nightmares.

Look, the clouds are shining again,
I creep on the wet ground, letting rain purify me
in the darkest mirrors early in the morning
when birds are bleeding and trees are talking.

I betrayed myself it scarred my skin, a scar
    so large
no one can see but me,
I should drown your expired body in the rain
so you'd vanish, like some slaughtered tree;

You would love it. Masochism was your only
    charm, darling.
Listen, I can hear the sun singing again
but it makes no difference; you abhor the sun
complaining it's too bright for your dead eyes.

The Darkness I Am Drowning in

Your hair is as dark as my thoughts and
it's streaming down your face, like tears and
blood of martyrs in a war against love.
Your cheekbones are the razors
suicidal poets use to cut their veins.

Your eyes are slanted and when I ask whether
    you have Asian heritage,
you suffice to say, 'Ancestry is French.'
which reminds me of
that scene in Godard's Contempt where
    Brigitte Bardot is addressed,
'Je t'aime totalement, tendrement,
    tragiquement.'

But I choke on these words and kiss your
    shadow, I

want you to worship me, hence I do not say
    anything.
Boy!
I know your soul is as dark as your hair
But your eyes are a stormy sea under generous
    sunrays

Your marble hands are as restless as my mind
I miss my routine,
I miss my ennui which you murdered
But the arrows of your energy are even more
    necessary than
the ecstasy of murder.

And the Ashes of Masculinity Will Melt in the Wind

My sister and I relish burning things we
    can't see
or feel. Last night we burnt God;
Today is the devil's turn;
Tomorrow we'll set fire
to all the one hundred and twenty-four
    thousand prophets.

Fox Flesh

Do you remember when I told you that I
    would kill my friends for you?
It gave you a thrill.
The sort of thrill that only blood induces
Hence I killed my friends and fried their
    floral flesh
served in fine china for dinner.

You ate it and complimented my cooking
your cheeks looked happier than ever
you said you were honoured and caressed my
    feet while crying
and I noticed your eyes were the bluest ocean
    that I
had ever drowned in. But then you said you
    had to leave.

Why did you leave?
I have been thinking, but I did not ask
instead I buried my trembling hands under
    the table
and tried my best to sound like my father,
to be my father;

I forced a smile and pressed my chin up like a
    hero, like my father.
My question choked me
I swallowed it down with vodka and it burnt
    my throat more than vodka
I don't think my father would be pleased if he
    saw me like this
He raised me to conquer, to question.

But I still wonder why you left;
I swam in you, I looked at you with my eyes
    closed,
I drew you on my bed and broke my plates.
My body was shaking when you were
    sipping beer,

I was waiting for you to finish your dinner, my
 mind was both rainy and sunny.

Someone was both screaming and singing in
 my anxious ears
was it my father warning me against your
 sunrays?
But I did not care I ignored my father — like all
 murderers do
I ignored my father for you but I didn't kill my
 friends for you
so, don't flatter yourself.

I killed my friends for the sake of murder
I killed them because I was bored with them
I killed them because I prefer to be friends
 with plants and rivers
because I can swim in a river
I can even drown myself in a river — if I want to.

I can do everything I want to, because that's
 what my father says

the next thing I want to do is to kill you
to cook you to eat you
and then sit in my sunny garden, feeling sorry
    for myself
that I shared the flesh of my friends with you
    — the most worthless fox in London.

Real Leeches

You don't see the leeches — they're on my back
black as my lips stuck on my brain
like my childhood nightmares drinking my
blood red shame.
You think my back is smooth
my love, you think I am smooth
you think my skin is as smooth as your
soul; you think my leeches never existed —
    or like God
they once did, but now, they're gone.

But my leeches are here, near, on my
skin, drinking my blue blood, my red thoughts,
my dark dreams, my morning decadance
you think they died with my mother, but
    my love
my leeches are right here, in my sleeves,

under my shirt on that body that you want to
    worship every violent night,
when you look closely you say there is nothing
    to see but
beauty. But my love, you can't be more wrong,
you can't be more blind.

My leeches are right here, close your eyes with
    me, pull up
my shirt, use your telescope and you will see.
And you will elope without me, from me,
because my leeches are real.

III Ode

I love you and I know you love me because
our love wraps around my body and it is the
warmest blanket I have ever had
even warmer than the duvet I had until
the age of nine which my dad laid on me
    every night.

The white duvet with miniatures of light blue
    and mint green bears
who sang to me until I dreamed of flying rabbits
your love is even softer and brighter than
    that duvet,
tender as summer on a humid island with dewy
    plants that emit the scent of your skin after
    your midnight bath and when I am in your
    arms, you sing to me, stroking my ears

I fall asleep dreaming of powerful mountains
     and my father.
I love your everything. I love your cooking
     because
you cook tasty dragons and rose rice for me,
     like my mum did
and I never expected to have the glorious taste
     of dragon's flesh in my mouth after
my mother's death, but I was wrong.

It would be cowardly to say I love you as I am
     in love with you
Not just because your name rhymes with 'rain'
     in my mother tongue, *baran*
but because I adore drowning in your
     oceanic eyes
and drowning used to be my phobia.
But you have to stop.

You shouldn't tell me, 'You have kissed
   someone else. That's why
you are sick; it is a virus.'
Because I cannot kiss anyone but you on the lips
the only arms I can fall asleep in belong to you
I belong to you and that is why I am ill.

Nothing is Wrong

In faded pictures. I recognise the sky of my city
burning with pollution melting in its
    aggressive sun,
violating its dark clouds. This sacred city
    of mine
slaughters its citizens with ancient religious
    laws. Blood-red threats from inside and out.

I remember its scorching summers wrapped
    in hijab
I recall its grey autumn showers resurrecting
    the naked trees
and its beautiful cafes as bright as the summer
    sky, smelling like
Masala tea, cardamom, saffron, cigarette smoke
    smelling like cinnamon thoughts.

I dream of my mother shopping in Tajrish
    square as though nothing were wrong,
Ahmad tea, Golestan rice, and colourful tank
    tops looking like blood-thirsty flags,
but smelling like organic olive oil. Perhaps,
    nothing was wrong.
But I know I'll always be sad, my sorrow is
    called Tehran.

Biography

Sogol Sur was born in 1988 in Tehran. After getting her BA in English Literature from Shahid Beheshti University, she came to London to study for an MA in Creative Writing at Birkbeck College, University of London. She has performed both her prose and poetry in numerous literary events in the UK. Her writing has appeared in Shout Out UK, The Writer's Hub, The Lion, Femmeuray, Confronting Rape Culture Chapbooks, and the Anthology. She is currently undertaking a PhD in Creative Writing at Birkbeck, whilst finishing her first collection of short stories. Both her creative and academic writing explore themes of queerness and hybridity.